IMAGES
of America
RIVERSIDE'S MISSION INN

COURTYARD VIEW, GLENWOOD MISSION INN HOTEL, 1905. As the writer of this postcard says, "Please come out and let me show you the place." This sentiment has been echoed perpetually throughout the history of the Mission Inn.

ON THE COVER: Mission Inn owner Frank Miller and his wife lead a group of early hotel guests for a day out in Southern California's sunshine. For over 100 years, the Mission Inn hotel in Riverside, California, has been an attraction for people who are amazed by its architecture, atmosphere, and collections.

IMAGES of America
RIVERSIDE'S MISSION INN

Steve Lech and Kim Jarrell Johnson

ARCADIA
PUBLISHING

Copyright © 2006 by Steve Lech and Kim Jarrell Johnson
ISBN 978-0-7385-4671-1

Published by Arcadia Publishing
Charleston SC, Chicago IL, Portsmouth NH, San Francisco CA

Printed in the United States of America

Library of Congress Catalog Card Number: 2006926312

For all general information contact Arcadia Publishing at:
Telephone 843-853-2070
Fax 843-853-0044
E-mail sales@arcadiapublishing.com
For customer service and orders:
Toll-Free 1-888-313-2665

Visit us on the Internet at www.arcadiapublishing.com

Contents

Acknowledgments 6

Introduction		7
1.	Before the Mission Inn (1873–1903)	9
2.	The Mission Wing (1903)	21
3.	The Cloister Wing (1911)	49
4.	The Spanish Wing (1914)	63
5.	The Rotunda Wing (1931)	75
6.	Faces at the Mission Inn	87
7.	The Mission Inn since Frank Miller	101
8.	The Miller Family	119
Bibliography		128

Acknowledgments

Several individuals and organizations contributed to this project. We would like to thank the Mission Inn Foundation for their support of this book from its inception. Steve Spiller, museum and collections manager, spent hours combing through the foundation's collections for us and answering our many questions. Steve Huffman, director of engineering for the Mission Inn hotel, generously shared his time, knowledge, and photographs of the hotel renovation. The Riverside Metropolitan Museum allowed us to use its collection of Miller family photographs, which added a great deal to this book. Kevin Hallaran, museum archivist, was both facilitator and helper, and we appreciate the time he spent on our behalf. We would also like to thank Catherine Manion, who shared the story of her mother as well as a photograph. Finally local historian and Mission Inn researcher Joan Hall contributed both her encouragement and several of her pictures. To all who encouraged this project and lent their support, we would like to give a heartfelt thank you.

INTRODUCTION

Riverside's historic Mission Inn hotel is an architectural wonder whose history closely follows that of the city in which it lies. From its humble beginnings as the Glenwood Hotel, a small cottage boardinghouse that served the needs of the modest agricultural colony, the Mission Inn grew out of the need to house (in "proper" quarters) the successive waves of very wealthy tourists coming to Riverside to see for themselves the potential riches that could be had with a few acres of producing Washington navel orange trees, water, and, of course, sunshine.

The story of the Mission Inn's birth began in 1874 when engineer/surveyor Christopher Columbus Miller arrived in Riverside from Tomah, Wisconsin. Miller had hired on as an engineer at the Temescal Tin Mine south of Riverside. Soon he began to construct what would become Riverside's Lower Canal.

Meanwhile, his wife, Mary, and their four children, Emma, 20; Frank, 17; Alice, 14; and Edward, 10, stayed behind in Wisconsin. Mary was in poor health and Christopher Miller was looking for a new place to settle that had a milder climate. Apparently he found Riverside to his liking, for he soon bought the block bounded by Main, Sixth, Orange, and Seventh Streets and sent for his family in the fall of 1874.

By the next year, the Miller family was ready to begin constructing their new home. This home was built with an adobe first floor and a wooden second floor. It had 12 rooms and was finished in July 1876. On November 22, 1876, the Miller's took in their first paying guest, Albert S. White, a wealthy man from New York, and the Glenwood Cottages guesthouse was born. The additional income from paying guests was welcomed by the family.

The new hotel was something of a success, and in 1878, with the help of his business partner and son-in-law Gustavus Newman, Miller constructed a new addition that included a dining room, kitchen, office, and some bedrooms. However, Christopher Miller soon grew tired of the rooming house business, and in February 1880, he sold the block of land and all structures to his oldest son Frank. The young Frank Miller paid $5,000—$2,500 down with a note for the rest, which he paid off in just one year. The year 1880 had one more milestone in the Miller family—the marriage of Frank Miller to Isabella Hardenburg, one of the first women schoolteachers in Riverside.

Frank Miller added to his hotel in 1882, and photographs from the time show he developed a large establishment with porches, balconies, and lushly landscaped grounds. However, Riverside's burgeoning orange orchards and subsequent wealth soon outpaced the small hotel and made Frank Miller realize that both he and Riverside needed a grand destination hotel, the type that would attract and retain visitors from the cold east and Midwest who would stay for months at a time. In the spring of 1894, he made a public announcement that he would build such a hotel in Riverside.

However, it took Frank Miller nearly 10 years to launch his idea for a world-class hotel. Idea after idea for financing fell through, but Frank kept trying to fulfill his dream. Finally, in 1902, a financing plan fell into place. The proposed hotel, which would cost $250,000, was to be partly funded with money from stock purchased by Frank's family and friends, as well as local townspeople.

The most significant investment came from Henry E. Huntington, a wealthy businessman who owned the Pacific Electric Company. He invested $75,000 in the new hotel, seeing it as an opportunity to expand his PE lines into inland Southern California.

The new hotel finally opened in January 1903. Christened the Glenwood Mission Inn, it was built in a Mission style of architecture that took advantage of the movement in California to preserve and enhance California's mission and Spanish history. Spearheaded by architect Arthur Benton, who designed the initial Glenwood Mission Inn hotel, the movement to replicate and preserve Mission architecture led to several buildings in Riverside and many more throughout Southern California. In the case of the Mission Inn, though, the fact that it was a hostelry that emulated the missions themselves led to rumors over the years that the Mission Inn (the Glenwood portion of the name was dropped by the 1930s) was once a California mission. However, the use of Mission architecture and Frank Miller's own dictum that "You cannot be both grand and comfortable" made the Mission Inn unique among large hotels of its time. Unlike others in the state, it was the one hotel that was uniquely Californian in style and architecture.

The Mission Inn quickly became a place of repose for the famous and wealthy alike. Businessmen, movie stars, aviation heroes, and many others from all walks of life soon made the Mission Inn the main attraction in Riverside. Over the next 30 years, Frank Miller added three wings—the Cloister, Spanish, and Rotunda—to the rear of the original mission wing so that by 1931, the hotel encompassed the entire block upon which it sits. Because he catered to a destination market of guests that would stay for extended lengths of time, he filled his hotel with artwork and statuary from around the world to provide diversion for his guests. Thus the hotel was from its very beginning, not just a hotel, but also a museum that enthralled its visitors.

June 1935 marked the end of an era when Frank Miller died. The Mission Inn was then taken over by his daughter Allis and her husband, DeWitt Hutchings, both of whom had helped to manage the hotel for several years. After their tenure ended in the early 1950s, the Mission Inn was sold to Ben Swig of the Fairmount Hotel in San Francisco, and then to a long list of parties whose interests lay not with the Inn. In 1969, the Friends of the Mission Inn formed to help save the aging structure. The City of Riverside purchased it in 1976 and formed the Mission Inn Foundation to oversee its operation. By 1985, it had been determined that the Mission Inn needed a complete renovation, and in that year, it was sold to the Carley Capital Group for just that purpose. The Mission Inn closed in June 1985 for what was to be a two-year renovation. Seven and a half years later, in December 1992, a renovated Mission Inn was purchased and reopened by local businessman and entrepreneur Duane R. Roberts, who has been referred to as the "Keeper of the Inn."

We hope that you will enjoy this trip through the history of this remarkable hotel. As a writer once stated in 1923, "Riverside is a city with a Mission Inn its heart." That statement rings just as true today as it did then.

One
BEFORE THE MISSION INN
1873–1903

AERIAL VIEW OF THE GLENWOOD, MID-1880S. The Glenwood Hotel was the precursor of the Mission Inn. It started as the private residence of the Christopher Miller family and later grew into the hotel seen here. The 1878 addition is to the right, and the 1882 addition is on the left. (Courtesy Riverside Metropolitan Museum.)

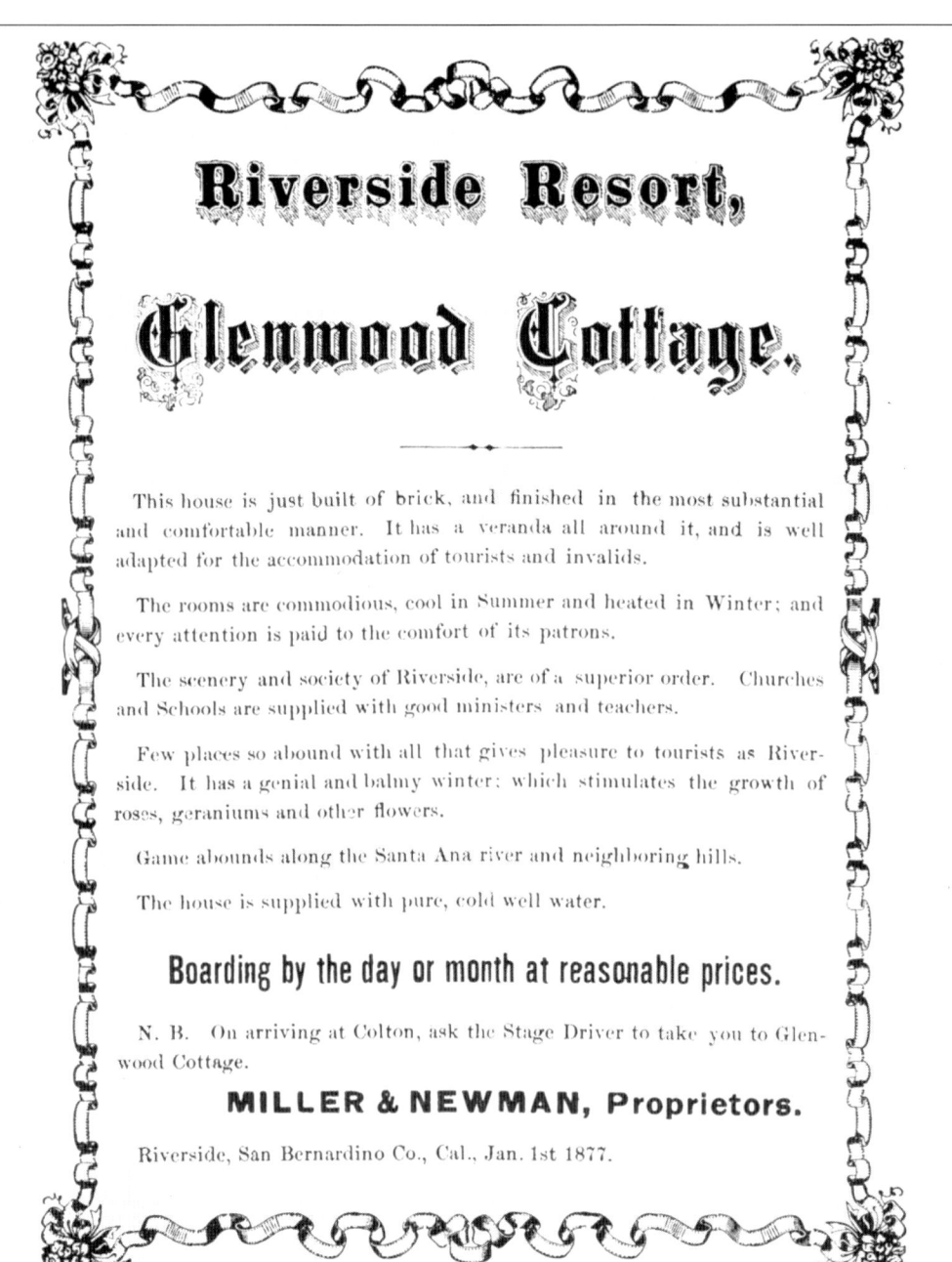

GLENWOOD HOTEL ADVERTISEMENT, 1877. This is one of the first Glenwood Hotel advertisements, published January 1, 1877. At that time, the Glenwood proprietors were Christopher Miller and his son-in-law Gustavus Newman. The advertisement points out the comfortable accommodations at the Glenwood and encourages both tourists and invalids to visit. Note the nearest train station at that time was Colton, and guests disembarking the train there were to "ask the Stage Driver to take you to Glenwood Cottage." (Courtesy Mission Inn Museum.)

STAGECOACH, C. 1883. The local stage, pictured here, connected Riverside to the nearest train station in Colton, which was about five miles away. The stage is pictured in front of the Miller family home, which was built of adobe and wood in 1875. By the time of this photograph, the home had been turned into part of the Glenwood Hotel. (Courtesy Mission Inn Museum.)

GLENWOOD HOTEL, MID-1880S. This photograph looks southeast and shows Main Street in the foreground. The 1878 addition to the hotel is to the left, and the 1882 addition, stretching to Main Street, is to the right. (Courtesy Mission Inn Museum.)

GLENWOOD HOTEL FROM SEVENTH STREET, MID-1880S. This photograph shows the Glenwood Hotel from Seventh Street (now Mission Inn Avenue). The people are on the porch of the 1882 addition, which was located west of the former Miller family home. (Courtesy Mission Inn Museum.)

DRAWING OF GLENWOOD HOTEL, 1883. This drawing of the Glenwood was used for several advertisements and was included in Wallace Elliot's 1883 *History of San Bernardino and San Diego Counties*. The view looks toward the northeast from Main Street. (Courtesy Mission Inn Museum.)

GUESTS ON THE GLENWOOD PORCH, 1880S. Guests of the Glenwood are relaxing on the porch of the hotel. In many instances, guests such as those pictured above would have been "wintering" in Southern California, escaping the harsh winters of the Midwest or East coast. (Courtesy Mission Inn Museum.)

MILLER FAMILY AND GUESTS, GLENWOOD HOTEL, SPRING 1884. By the time of this photograph, Frank Miller (standing on the left) had assumed ownership of the Glenwood. Frank Richardson, the husband of Frank Miller's sister Alice, is pictured to the right of the photograph, seated next to the baby carriage. He was the day-to-day manager of the hotel. (Courtesy Riverside Metropolitan Museum.)

MAIN STREET VIEW, C. 1885. Looking south on Main Street, the Glenwood Hotel is on the left. This photograph was obviously taken to show the boy with the cannon in the center. It may have been part of a function for a veteran's group, such as the Grand Army of the Republic, which was quite active in Riverside. (Courtesy Riverside Metropolitan Museum.)

ORANGE DAY, 1895. The Glenwood celebrated Orange Day in Riverside in 1895 by creating this display made out of oranges on the hotel lawn. Riverside was the center of a premier navel orange growing region, and Frank Miller did his utmost to boost citrus and Riverside. (Courtesy Mission Inn Museum.)

INSIDE THE GLENWOOD HOTEL, 1880S. The above left photograph shows the parlor and the above right photograph shows the dining room of the Glenwood Hotel. Both rooms exhibit the comfortable, home-like atmosphere for which the Glenwood was famous. The Glenwood was considered a cottage-type hotel that was appropriate for Riverside in the 1870s and 1880s.

However, by the 1890s, Riverside had become a very wealthy city due to the navel orange industry and needed more luxurious accommodations for the rich tourists and investors who visited the area. (Both courtesy Riverside Metropolitan Museum.)

GLENWOOD HOTEL GUEST REGISTER, 1886. This page, dated January 4, 1886, is from the guest register at the Glenwood Hotel. The seventh signature from the top is Charles Chaffey, one of the Chaffey brothers who founded and developed the city of Ontario, California. Note also Frank Miller's signature on his own ledger. (Courtesy Mission Inn Museum.)

GLENWOOD HOTEL PERGOLA, 1902. This May 1902 photograph shows a red-tile roofed pergola near the dining room at the Glenwood hotel. Even before the construction of the Mission Inn, Frank Miller was incorporating Mission-style architectural elements into the Glenwood Hotel. (Courtesy Riverside Metropolitan Museum.)

WHITE AND MILLER OFFICE, C. 1890. For a while, Frank Miller was in the insurance and real estate business with his mentor, Albert S. White, a local business leader. White was also the first guest to stay in the Glenwood Hotel. This view shows their office, located in the Oppenheimer Building on the west side of Main Street between Eighth Street (now University Avenue) and Ninth Street. (Courtesy Mission Inn Museum.)

PROPOSED NEW GLENWOOD HOTEL, 1894. In 1894, Frank Miller made the first announcement that he would replace his small hostelry with a grand hotel. The drawing pictured above is his original concept, based on the Hotel Colorado in Glenwood Springs, Colorado. As can be seen, this concept looks much more like the grand hotels of the East and Midwest. However, in the nearly 10 years it would take Frank Miller to secure funding for his new hotel, he realized that in order for it to be a uniquely California hotel, he would need to construct it to resemble a California mission and take advantage of a wave of nostalgia for the old Spanish days of California. Thus would be born the Mission Inn known and remembered today. (Courtesy Riverside Metropolitan Museum.)

Two
THE MISSION WING
1903

GLENWOOD MISSION INN OPENING DAY, FEBRUARY 20, 1903. "The new Glenwood Hotel was gorgeous in flags and bunting today, on the occasion of the formal opening of the big hostelry." The new hotel's grand opening was cause for celebration in Riverside, as the wealthy town now had a formal, luxury hotel with which to greet its many tourists. Members of the public were invited to inspect the new building, and all were impressed with Frank Miller's dream. (Courtesy Mission Inn Museum.)

TWO VIEWS OF THE MISSION WING, EARLY 1900S. The top view is artist William Alexander Sharp's sketch of architect Arthur Benton's new Glenwood Hotel, while the bottom is a postcard view from around 1905. The Glenwood Mission Inn opened to guests in January 1903 with the arrival of one of the famed Raymond excursion parties from the East. The wealthy easterners admired the hotel, which included a spacious lobby and meeting area, formal dining room, several ground-floor suites, and 275 rooms in the three upper levels. Having been built to resemble the early Spanish missions of California, the Mission Inn (the Glenwood name was dropped by the 1930s) soon became a popular tourist destination hotel and a luxury hotel that was unique among the many other hotels of that caliber in Southern California. (Above courtesy Mission Inn Museum; below courtesy Steve Lech.)

CONSTRUCTION OF THE MISSION WING, 1902. Construction of the Mission Wing began in 1902 with great fanfare—Riverside, after several years of indecision, was finally to have a grand hotel. In these two views, the brick foundations are being laid on the eastern portion of the building. The top view is looking from the courtyard toward the east (note the 1902 Carnegie library under construction in the background). The bottom view is looking west from Orange Street. (Both courtesy Riverside Metropolitan Museum.)

COURTYARD AND PERGOLA, 1904. Most first-class destination hotels of the era had a spacious courtyard, and the Mission Inn was no exception. Guests were typically coming to Riverside for several weeks or months at a time. Because most of them were coming to enjoy the climate, an outdoor courtyard was a must, and many afternoons would be spent here reading, relaxing, chatting with friends, playing games, etc. The pergola (a vine-covered structure to the right of the photograph) offered a shaded walkway for those who wanted it. (Courtesy Riverside Metropolitan Museum.)

CAMPANARIO AND OLD ADOBE, C. 1903. The campanario and "Old Adobe" were two very prominent fixtures in the courtyard of the new hotel. The campanario, or bell tower, was loosely patterned after the bell tower found on the Mission San Gabriel. This housed several bells and, as in this photograph, a small girl sitting in a niche looking at the camera. The "Old Adobe" was simply the old Miller home with modifications. Instead of tearing the whole structure down as he originally wanted, Frank Miller took only the second floor off and converted the building into a cozy room that could be used for meetings, afternoon teas, reading, etc. (Courtesy Mission Inn Museum.)

MISSION INN ESCUTCHEON, C. 1910. The escutcheon was a compendium of symbols put together by William Sharp to advertise the Mission Inn and further the symbolism of the new hotel. At the top is the raincross figure devised for the hotel by Frank Miller. It consists of a two-tiered cross over a mission bell in its frame. This symbol became so popular that it was later adopted by the city of Riverside. The figure on the left is St. Francis, patron saint of the hotel, and Fr. Junipero Serra is on the right. Below is a California American Indian. The Inn's motto, "Enter, this is your home, friend," is rendered in Spanish to complete the escutcheon. (Courtesy Steve Lech.)

OLD ADOBE AND COURTYARD, C. 1905. "Where stood the hut in that wild land / The Mission Inn stands fair and grand, / Like ancient mission hostelry, / With every modern courtesy, / Of builder's art for comfort's sake / Wherein the old time art should take / Thoughts backward to the restful time / Of California's maiden prime. / Then plans were drawn by he who drew / Was one who well the Missions knew." (Courtesy Mission Inn Museum.)

INTERIOR, OLD ADOBE, C. 1905. This room had been the parlor of the Miller home but after construction of the Mission Inn became a meeting room, of sorts. Note the collection of American Indian baskets combined with the eclectic mix of various styles of furniture, which became a trademark of the Mission Inn. Riverside's Aurantia chapter of the DAR conducted their first meeting in this room in 1905. (Courtesy Mission Inn Museum.)

CORNER, OLD ADOBE TEA ROOM, C. 1915. This is the entrance to the tearoom from the pergola. This and many other views were photograph cards, printed en masse and sold in the Inn's gift store in later years. (Courtesy Riverside Metropolitan Museum.)

ARCHES OF THE MISSION INN, C. 1910. In 1908, in order to create a larger street presence for his hotel, Frank Miller commissioned architect Arthur Benton to design and build an arched arcade along the Seventh Street entrance to the new hotel. These arches, patterned after arched arcades at many California missions, were built in 1908 and furthered the mission ambience that Miller desired. (Courtesy Steve Lech.)

INTERIOR VIEW, MISSION INN ARCHES, C. 1925. By the time this photograph was taken, vines had covered the arches, the landscaping in the courtyard had matured, and the courtyard of the Mission Inn had become a more private location to relax. The entry drive also became more auto-accessible, as illustrated by the presence of the car on the left. This driveway remains today. (Courtesy Riverside Metropolitan Museum.)

DECORATION DAY CELEBRATIONS, 1913 AND 1914. The new Mission Inn soon became the center of activity in Riverside. It hosted banquets, club meetings, special dinners, and various celebrations. Pictured here are two Decoration Day celebrations (1913 above and 1914 below) sponsored by the Grand Army of the Republic, an organization composed of Union Civil War Veterans whose Riverside chapter was very active in town until the 1920s. Decoration Day is known today as Memorial Day. (Above courtesy Riverside Metropolitan Museum; below courtesy Joan Hall.)

QUIET AREA IN THE COURTYARD, C. 1915. The courtyard offered places to sit and stroll and offered many curiosities about which people could wonder. Here we see two swings offered for the enjoyment of the guests. (Courtesy Steve Lech.)

GUESTS SEATED IN THE COURTYARD, C. 1912. These two ladies are enjoying a quiet moment in the Mission Inn courtyard. Most of the guests at the Mission Inn were "wintering" in Southern California, spending several weeks and even months at the Mission Inn. This made for a hectic tourist season between October and April. During the rest of the year, Frank Miller and his family would travel throughout the world collecting artifacts for the hotel. (Courtesy Mission Inn Museum.)

EL RINCON DE CASTILLO FOUNTAIN, 1920S. This set of artificial rocks and basin was the largest fountain at the Mission Inn. It was (and still is) located along Seventh Street just next to the main entrance. Emulating the tradition of the Trevi Fountain in Rome, it was the custom of guests who wished to return someday to the Mission Inn to drop a coin in the basin of the fountain. (Courtesy Mission Inn Museum.)

ST. CATHERINE'S WELL AND OLD ADOBE, C. 1910. St. Catherine's Well was another bit of decoration to adorn the Court of the Birds. It was not an actual well, but a drinking fountain (Note the faucet and mugs visible on top). Similarly, it was not actually named for a real St. Catherine. It apparently was named for an early and frequent hotel guest. St. Catherine's Well still stands near the main entrance to the hotel. (Courtesy Riverside Metropolitan Museum.)

NAPOLEON AND JOSEPH, C. 1920S. Napoleon and Joseph were two large macaws that lived in the Mission Inn courtyard for many years. Because of them, the area was and still is generally known as the Court of the Birds. Napoleon's name comes from that fact that his blue and yellow plumage resembled the uniform worn by Emperor Napoleon, whereas Joseph's "coat of many colors" earned him his name. These two birds were a popular attraction to Inn guests, many of whom had never seen a tropical bird before. The macaws were known for entertaining guests, eating out of their hands, and occasionally whistling at women passing by, much to the consternation of any nearby man thought to be the perpetrator. (Courtesy Steve Lech.)

TWO VIEWS OF THE NANKING BELL, C. 1915. Bells held a special place for Frank Miller and his family, and over the years, they collected several hundred of them. Of all of them, the Nanking bell is the largest in the Inn's collection. It is over six feet high and weighs one to one-and-a-half tons. It is Chinese in origin, having hung in the temple of the Manchu in the center of Nanking, where government officials resided during the days of the Empire. The temple was destroyed during the revolution of 1912, and the bell was moved and eventually came into the possession of Frank Miller. In the above view, the bell is in its place in front of the old adobe, while in the view to the right, guest Maude Fellows enjoys the Riverside sunshine against the backdrop of the large bell. (Courtesy Mission Inn Museum.)

AGUA MANSA BELL. This bell was originally part of the Agua Mansa church near Colton and most likely dates to around 1851. In May 1918, Frank Miller purchased it from the parishioners of the church of the Holy Rosary in south Colton to add to his bell collection. The old church had burned, and the bell would not fit into the new church. Miller paid $500 for the old bell and purchased a replacement for the new church. (Courtesy Mission Inn Museum.)

ADVERTISING CART FOR RAMONA PAGEANT, 1923. This cart was driven throughout the inland area to garner support for the first season of Hemet's Ramona Pageant. The oft-told story of Ramona inspired people like Arthur Benton and Frank Miller to build structures resembling the missions and haciendas of California's past, and it was fitting that the cart would make a stop in the courtyard of the Mission Inn. (Courtesy Mission Inn Museum.)

THE MISSION INN

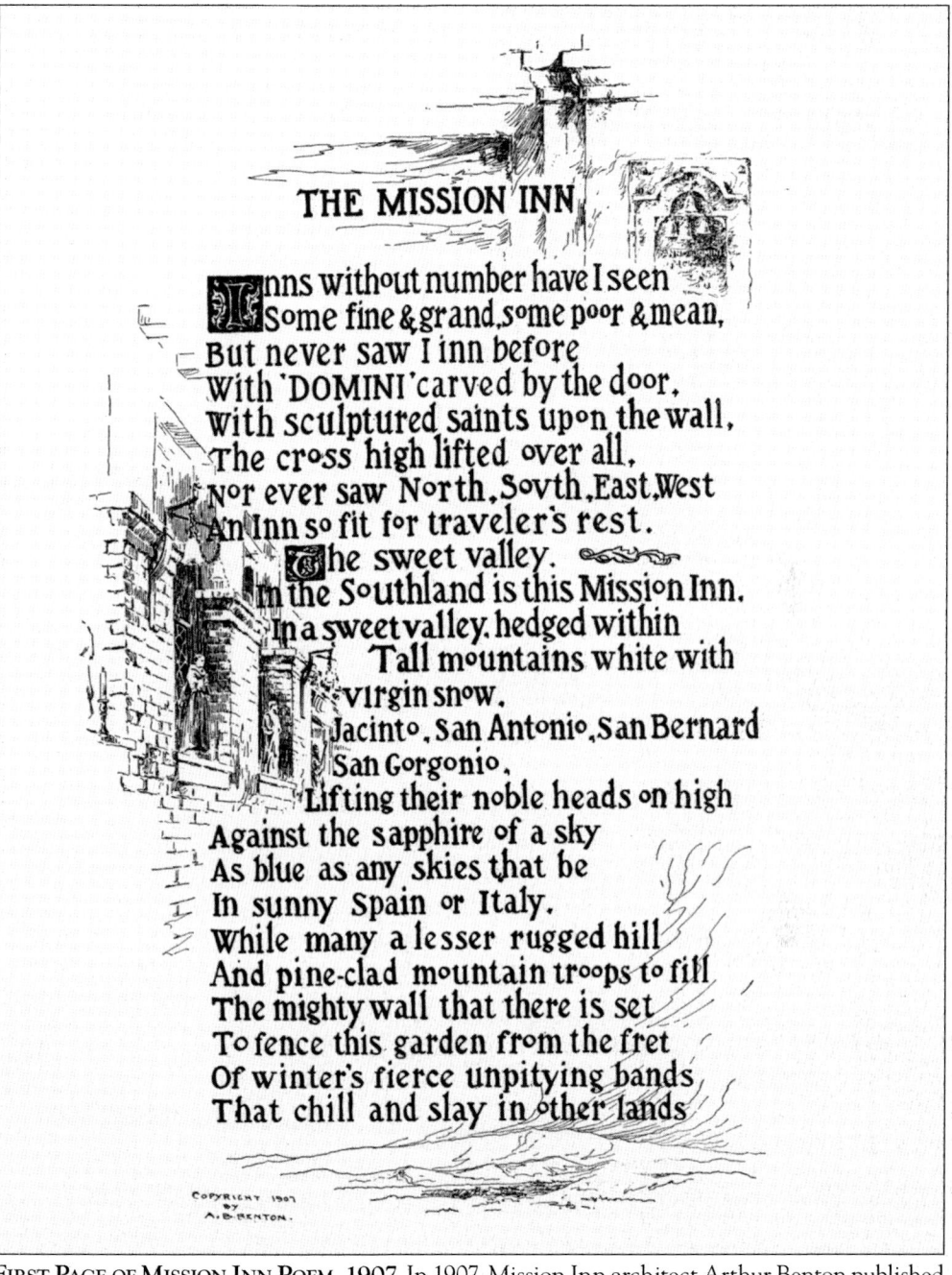

Inns without number have I seen
Some fine & grand, some poor & mean,
But never saw I inn before
With 'DOMINI' carved by the door,
With sculptured saints upon the wall,
The cross high lifted over all,
Nor ever saw North, South, East, West
An Inn so fit for traveler's rest.
The sweet valley.
In the Southland is this Mission Inn.
In a sweet valley, hedged within
Tall mountains white with
virgin snow.
Jacinto, San Antonio, San Bernard
San Gorgonio,
Lifting their noble heads on high
Against the sapphire of a sky
As blue as any skies that be
In sunny Spain or Italy.
While many a lesser rugged hill
And pine-clad mountain troops to fill
The mighty wall that there is set
To fence this garden from the fret
Of winter's fierce unpitying bands
That chill and slay in other lands

COPYRIGHT 1907
BY
A. B. BENTON.

FIRST PAGE OF MISSION INN POEM, 1907. In 1907, Mission Inn architect Arthur Benton published a book-length poem about the Inn, the missions, and Riverside. William Sharp illustrated it throughout with line drawings of many aspects of the new hotel. In it, Benton said of Frank Miller and the Inn: "So spread the Glenwood's name / Came tens, then scores, then hundreds came: / Then he who as a lad had filled / The moulds with clay with which to build / His fathers house, now dreamed that he / The builder of an Inn would be / Like ancient mission hostelry, / With every modern courtesy / Of builder's art for comfort's sake / Wherein the old time art should take / Thoughts backward to the restful time / Of California's maiden prime." (Courtesy Steve Lech.)

EL PASEO DE LAS PALMAS, C. 1905. Benton's poem describes this area, located on top of the Mission Wing: "And higher up a parapet / With balustrade wherein are set / Great pots where flowers luxuriant show. / And palms in long perspective grow. / A roof walk backed by sunny rooms, / Deep arches filled with choicest blooms, / Tiled roofs with gables quaint & high, / And one great tower against the sky. / No architectural pomp is here, / But simple forms & lines severe. / Yet o'er the whole is written plain / The subtle art of ancient Spain." (Courtesy Mission Inn Museum.)

MISSION INN GUESTS, 1912. As can be seen by the clothes worn by these three guests, staying at the Mission Inn was a formal affair, with people even dressing up for a morning in the sunshine. This view is looking southeast, with the campanario off to the right. (Courtesy Mission Inn Museum.)

VIEW OF PERGOLA, C. 1907. The pergola was a covered walkway that lined the interior of the courtyard, as it does today. Later Frank Miller tried to continue the pergola from the hotel down to the train stations at Seventh and Vine Streets. Although several portions were completed (as seen today along Seventh Street east of Lime Street), it never quite made a continuous run from the depots to the hotel. (Courtesy Riverside Metropolitan Museum.)

LOBBY AND FRONT DESK, C. 1910. This scene is what first greeted the visitor upon entering the Mission Inn. It is easy to see how the hotel was termed "eclectic" in the early years. There were Arts and Crafts style chairs, Navaho rugs, lamps on chains, and a whole assortment of various bric-a-brac to entice the eyes. The sign in the upper left corner reads, "Ye canna expect to be baith grand and comfortable" and symbolizes Frank Miller's ideas about hospitality. Although the Mission Inn was a modern, luxury hotel, it was not grand in the sense of having marble floors, towering columns, and the various other trappings of Victorian-era hotels. The Mission Inn was meant to be modern yet comfortable—an updated version of the missions themselves. Frank Miller's sister Alice Richardson, longtime manager of the hotel, stands in the center, ready to great new guests while Southern California booster Charles Fletcher Lummis stands at the front desk. (Courtesy Mission Inn Museum.)

INGLENOOK, C. 1910. The Inglenook was originally a room behind the front desk. It also housed an eclectic collection of things and served as a room of relaxation. According to the Mission Inn's handbook, "The yawning fireplace, with its ruddy, crackling blaze, is a good thing to look at . . . and think meanwhile of the many varieties of snow, ice, sleet, hail, slush, mud, frost, wind, etc., that the folks are getting "back home." (Courtesy Mission Inn Museum.)

MISSION INN LOBBY, C. 1908. This area, to the east of the front desk, would have served as the sitting parlor in the early days. It could have been used by guests for relaxing during inclement weather, or after dark. Note the small orchestra stage on the right, which was used for small performances. Today the stage serves as the landing from the Orange Street entrance to the hotel. (Courtesy Steve Lech.)

St. Francis Doors. The St. Francis doors open into the California Dining Room from the main hotel lobby. The doors consist of several panels that highlight scenes from the life of St. Francis. Most of the panels were handwrought by resident metalworker Archibald Barrelle, said to be a pupil of St. Gaudens. Thyrsis Field and Albert Stahler contributed also, as did W. R. Elfers, who created the intricate open screens depicting birds. (Courtesy Mission Inn Museum.)

California Dining Room, c. 1912. The California Room was the main dining room in the hotel. Entered just off the lobby, it was where the guests ate all of their meals while staying at the Mission Inn. As was customary for the time, mealtimes were formal affairs, as evidenced by the waitstaff in starched white uniforms. (Courtesy Mission Inn Museum.)

EASTER DECORATION IN THE MAIN DINING ROOM

California Dining Room, c. 1915. For special occasions, the California Dining Room was often decorated with bunting, palm fronds, or other items. This photograph shows the room prepared for an Easter meal, undoubtedly awaiting the arrival of guests who were at the Easter sunrise service on Mount Rubidoux. The use of "tropical" plants, such as palms, reinforced the fact that the Mission Inn's guests were in a region touted for its Mediterranean climate. These almost constant reminders added to the allure of the area and convinced many of them to buy land, build a home, and stay permanently. (Courtesy Mission Inn Museum.)

MIDDAY MEAL

March 27, 1916

Consomme Hot or Cold   Cream of Corn

California Ripe Olives
Radishes

Tenderloin of Sea Bass, Ravigote
Potato Chips

Hot Snails   Raisin Bread

Roast Lamb, Mint or Brown Sauce
Honeycomb Tripe, Gladstone
Poached Egg, Bearnaise

Baked Potatoes   Potatoes au Gratin
Hubbard Squash   Stewed Tomatoes

COLD SERVICE

Roast Beef   Ham   Tongue
Corned Beef   Booth Sardines   Salami

Beet and Watercress Salad   Lettuce, Mayonnaise

Green Apple Pie   Marmalade Tarts

Satsuma Plum Ice   Cake

Jonathan Apples   Grape Fruit Slices   Navel Oranges

California Peaches in Syrup

California and Swiss Cheese
Crackers

Buttermilk   Orangeade
Coffee   Tea   Iced Tea
Hollow-Hill Farm Certified Milk

Afternoon tea will be served in the Adobe between 4 and 6 p. m.

Cathedral Organ Music, 11½, 5 and 8 p. m.

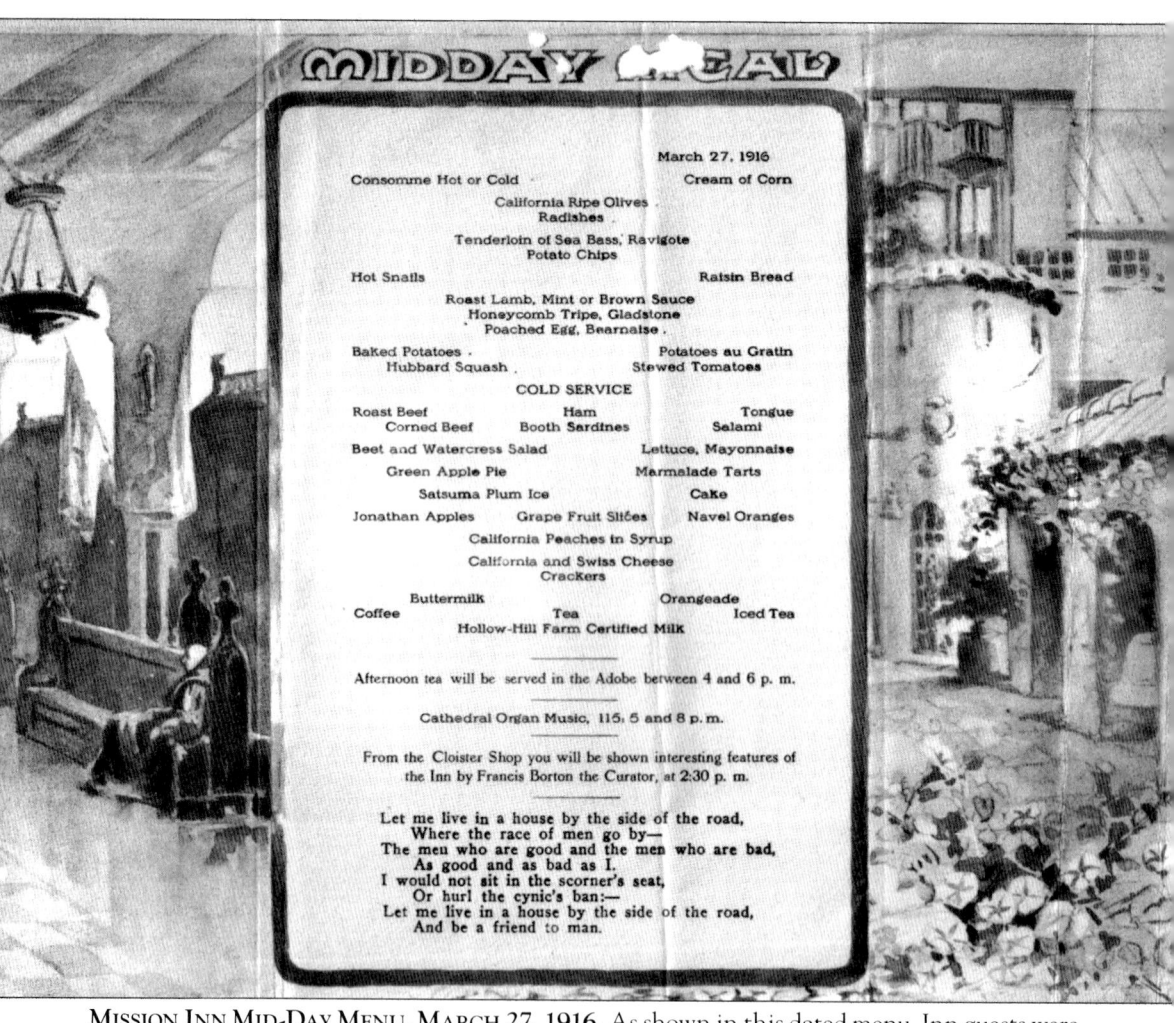

From the Cloister Shop you will be shown interesting features of the Inn by Francis Borton the Curator, at 2:30 p. m.

Let me live in a house by the side of the road,
   Where the race of men go by—
The men who are good and the men who are bad,
   As good and as bad as I.
I would not sit in the scorner's seat,
   Or hurl the cynic's ban:—
Let me live in a house by the side of the road,
   And be a friend to man.

MISSION INN MID-DAY MENU, MARCH 27, 1916. As shown in this dated menu, Inn guests were treated to a constantly changing variety of menu selections, many of which highlighted Southern California's agricultural specialties. (Courtesy Mission Inn Museum.)

MISSION INN DRAWING POSTCARD, 1930S. Sayings such as this one were popular with Frank Miller and were therefore used throughout his advertising. The drawings, which include various scenes from the Mission Inn over time, were drawn by architect Arthur Benton and resident artist William Sharp. (Courtesy Steve Lech.)

PRESIDENT TAFT'S CHAIR, 1910S. On October 12, 1909, Pres. William Howard Taft made a whirlwind tour of Redlands, San Bernardino, and Riverside. Having seen Riverside's orange groves along Magnolia and Victoria Avenues, the president was brought to the Mission Inn where he attended a banquet in his honor. To honor his important guest, Frank Miller commissioned this special chair for the large president. Although Taft sat in the chair for the banquet, its extreme size offended the president, and he would not allow his picture to be taken in it. Undaunted, Frank Miller placed the chair in the lobby, where it has remained ever since as one of the most popular artifacts at the hotel. (Courtesy Mission Inn Museum.)

PRESIDENTIAL SUITE, C. 1910. At the time of the Inn's opening, this suite was the largest in the hotel. Less than three months after the grand opening, Pres. Theodore Roosevelt was making a tour throughout Southern California and planned to visit Riverside. On May 7, 1903, he was taken on a quick tour of the town, followed by a night's rest at the new Glenwood Mission Inn. The president was given this suite, which soon after became known as the Presidential Suite in honor of his visit. Later a stained-glass window with the presidential flag and the date of 1903 was installed to commemorate this presidential visit. Today this room is known as the Presidential Lounge. (Courtesy Mission Inn Museum.)

MISSION INN EXCURSIONS. Because guests stayed for several weeks or months, hotels such as the Mission Inn had to provide recreational opportunities for guests. It was not uncommon to have poetry and/or scripture readings, musical recitals, plays, games (such as bowling, billiards, or tennis), or lectures of general interest. However, what really interested people were the various excursions that took place. These two photographs show the beginnings of such excursions, c. 1905 (above) and 1923 (below). Miller regularly took guests up Mount Rubidoux, along Magnolia and Victoria Avenues to examine the vast tracts of orange groves, or to either Fairmount or Chemawa Parks. These diversions provided a pleasant day out in the sunshine and were remembered for years afterward by many of the participants. (Courtesy Mission Inn Museum.)

California's Mission Hotel
THE GLENWOOD
Riverside, California

The Court and Campanile—The Glenwood

The most novel and attractive hotel in California. Located on all railroads.

In the Center of America's Most Productive Orange Belt

In its unique individuality THE GLENWOOD stands entirely alone.

Under the Pergola—The Glenwood

FRANK A. MILLER, Proprietor
MRS. F. W. RICHARDSON, Manager

GLENWOOD MISSION INN MAGAZINE ADVERTISEMENT, 1907. Frank Miller did extensive advertising for the hotel from the onset. The Mission Inn catered primarily to wealthy Eastern tourists, and so most of the advertisements such as the one above were found in literary magazines, society magazines, and other journals that catered to the traveling public. Note that the Inn is advertised as the most novel and attractive hotel in California and that it was located on all railroads—a definite plus in 1907. (Courtesy Steve Lech.)

Three
THE CLOISTER WING
1911

CLOISTER WING ADDITION, C. 1912. The Cloister Wing (originally called the Monastery) is the second of the four wings that make up the Mission Inn. Built between 1909 and 1911, it opened in July 1911 to great fanfare. In addition to adding some 45 hotel rooms, the Cloister contained the popular Music Room and a skating rink/tennis court on the roof. (Courtesy Steve Lech.)

CONSTRUCTION OF THE CLOISTER WING, 1910. Instead of romanticizing the architecture of the missions as the Mission Wing did, the Cloister copied them. The buttresses along Orange Street are copied from those at Mission San Gabriel, while the flying buttresses over the sidewalk are said to be patterned after a Texas mission. Similarly, the facade along Sixth Street is a stretched view of the Mission San Carlos Borromeo (Carmel) chapel facade. The scaffolding in the photograph above is allowing the construction of the Carmel Tower. (Courtesy Mission Inn Museum.)

CLOISTER WING VIEW, C. 1912. Frank Miller's use of Mission architecture led many to believe that the Mission Inn was one of the original California missions. Letters of inquiry to the hotel were often addressed to "The Rev. Father." This perception still exists—Mission Inn docents regularly surprise tour guests with the revelation that the Mission Inn has never been anything other than a hotel. (Courtesy Mission Inn Museum.)

INTERIOR VIEW, CLOISTER WING ROOM, C. 1930. This photograph shows the interior of a typical room on the Orange Street side. Note the writing nook on the left. It is housed inside the buttress, and to the right of it is a small balcony. The two ladies are Jessie van Brunt and her sister Carrie. Jessie van Brunt was a resident artist who specialized in stained-glass windows. (Courtesy Mission Inn Museum.)

CLOISTER MUSIC ROOM, C. 1915. The Music Room served as the main gathering place for Frank Miller and his guests. As the name implies, the room was used for concerts, recitals, plays, lectures, and other pastimes that were normal fare for destination hotels of the day. The balcony on the left and the ceiling above are patterned after the same at Mission San Miguel. Note the St. Cecilia windows above the stage and the organ to the right. (Courtesy Mission Inn Museum.)

MUSIC ROOM INTERIOR VIEW, 1912. This view is looking down into the Music Room from the balcony. Note the many flags and other items on the walls. Most of the larger rooms soon became display rooms for Frank Miller's growing collection of "stuff," as he put it. Note also the gargoyle on the steps. It was originally a water spout on the battlement of a Spanish castle near Barcelona. This is now part of the fountain in the Spanish Patio area. (Courtesy Riverside Metropolitan Museum.)

GIRL IN MUSIC ROOM, C. 1915. This girl is enjoying a relaxing moment in the back of the Music Room, perhaps even wondering at the extent of various artifacts on display. (Courtesy Mission Inn Museum.)

ST. CECILIA WINDOWS. St. Cecilia is the patron saint of music, which is appropriate for the Music Room. However, these windows had another meaning. They were commissioned as a memorial to Isabella Miller, who is pictured in the center as St. Cecilia, surrounded by various monks and nuns, several of Riverside's famed orange trees, the campanario in the courtyard, and the "Old Adobe." These three noticeable windows were built by Henry Eldridge Goodhue in his studios in Cambridge, Massachusetts. (Courtesy Riverside Metropolitan Museum.)

MUSIC ROOM PAGEANT, 1920s. Plays and other performances were held in the Music Room as part of the ongoing entertainment offered to the guests and residents of Riverside. Besides the one pictured above, there was an annual Christmas pageant and various other smaller performances. (Courtesy Riverside Metropolitan Museum.)

VIEW FROM MUSIC ROOM STAGE, 1912. This photograph is taken from the stage of the Music Room looking toward the balcony. Just to the right of the photograph was the entrance to the St. Cecilia Chapel, which was the first true wedding chapel at the Mission Inn. Until the early 1930s, the Music Room and St. Cecilia Chapel were used extensively for weddings. (Courtesy Riverside Metropolitan Museum.)

MUSIC ROOM PIPE ORGAN, C. 1920. For over 25 years, the Mission Inn was the only luxury hotel in California to have its own pipe organ. Constructed by the Kimball Company, the organ was incorporated into the building of the Music Room and offered many years of recitals, concerts, and other events. Beginning in 2000, the Friends of the Mission Inn funded a complete restoration of the organ, and now it is frequently played at various occasions. (Courtesy Mission Inn Museum.)

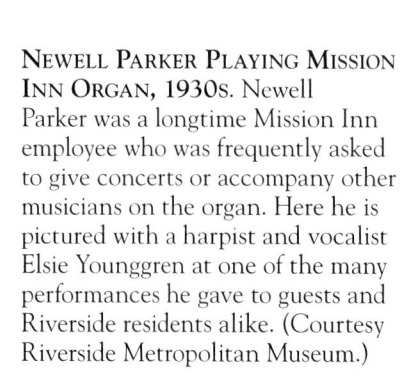

NEWELL PARKER PLAYING MISSION INN ORGAN, 1930s. Newell Parker was a longtime Mission Inn employee who was frequently asked to give concerts or accompany other musicians on the organ. Here he is pictured with a harpist and vocalist Elsie Younggren at one of the many performances he gave to guests and Riverside residents alike. (Courtesy Riverside Metropolitan Museum.)

CLOISTER WALK, C. 1920. The Cloister Walk was added shortly after the construction of the Cloister Wing and consisted of a series of tunnels and small rooms running generally along the Orange Street side of the building. This area became a showplace for many of Frank Miller's treasures and, in later years, when it was renamed the Catacombs, was the focus of much of the Inn's lore. These tunnels exist only on Mission Inn property and do not extend to other buildings downtown. (Courtesy Steve Lech.)

REFECTORIO, EARLY 1920S. The Refectorio (refectory in English) was a room located directly under the Music Room stage. This room served as a sitting room, a display room, and as a small, private meeting room for committees and organizations on occasion. The Cloister Walk could be accessed through the Refectorio. The windows pictured on the right were designed by resident artist William Sharp. (Courtesy Mission Inn Museum.)

PAPAL COURT DISPLAY, C. 1918. While at the 1915 Pan-Pacific Exposition in San Francisco, Frank Miller purchased this display of the papal court of Pius X and his attendants. These wax and paper mache figures were housed in a special room at the far end of the Cloister Walk and were on display for many years. A few of them can still be seen in the Mission Inn Museum. (Courtesy Mission Inn Museum.)

SANTA CLARA CHAPEL, C. 1918. This small chapel was named for St. Clara, a contemporary of St. Francis of Assisi. The figure of St. Clara on the altar is Spanish, from about 1650. The altar itself is of San Antonio de Padua. Above this in the small box is a figure of the Christ child, surrounded by cherubs. The prayer wheel is Italian, probably from the 1700s. (Courtesy Mission Inn Museum.)

ST. CECILIA ROOM, C. 1912. This was a room just off the Music Room stage that was dedicated to displaying several musical objects. The pianoforte on the right was made in Seville in 1788 by the purveyor to the royal family, while the windows were designed by artist John La Forge, who developed what was termed "opalescent glass." Many such rooms, all housing various collections, could be found throughout the Mission Inn. (Courtesy Joan Hall.)

CLOISTER ART SHOP, LATE 1910S. The Cloister Art Shop was the Mission Inn's version of a gift and curio shop. In it, guests could purchase not only postcards, pamphlets, brochures, and other ephemera about the hotel but also any one of many antiquities and objects d'art that Frank Miller had procured abroad, shipped back home, and then decided to sell. As seen in this photograph, there were many things from which to choose. (Courtesy Riverside Metropolitan Museum.)

The Garden of the Bells, Glenwood Mission Inn, Riverside, California.

GARDEN OF THE BELLS, 1912. The Garden of the Bells was added as part of the Cloister Wing and was meant as a sitting and relaxation area. True to the Cloister Wing, the Garden of the Bells emulates existing Mission architecture. The large bell tower on the left is copied from the one at the Pala Assistencia near Temecula, and the arched arcade is reminiscent of the one found at Mission San Juan Capistrano. Note the west side of the Cloister Wing in the back. When originally built, it was plain. However, Frank Miller's desire to continuously change the Mission Inn by adding and redecorating would later result in the placement of several tile mosaics and statues on the walls and the addition of two rooms on the top of the building, as can be seen today. (Courtesy Steve Lech.)

GARDEN OF THE BELLS, C. 1930. Many bells within the Inn's collection were displayed in the Garden of the Bells. The Millers' collection of bells became known worldwide, and several important specimens were donated to them over the years, including the first locomotive bell heard in Riverside. (Courtesy Mission Inn Museum.)

OLDEST DATED CHRISTIAN BELL, 1930S. This Spanish bell, dated 1247, is the oldest dated bell in the Christian world. Frank Miller procured it from the shop of the bell maker who cast London's Big Ben. It hangs on the southernmost portion of the arcade that makes up the Garden of the Bells. To get a true idea of the age of this bell, at the time it was cast, Louis IX of France was preparing for the sixth crusade. (Courtesy Mission Inn Museum.)

THE ALHAMBRA SUITE, LATE 1920S. The Alhambra Suite was added on top of the Cloister Wing. For many years, this was the largest suite in the hotel. Constructed in a Moorish style, it had a huge fireplace and boasted of beams made of fragrant Mexican cedar. Writer Hamlin Garland spent many weeks in the Alhambra during his later years. Just outside of the Alhambra Suite is the Alhambra Court. (Courtesy Mission Inn Museum.)

ALHAMBRA COURT, C. 1930. The Alhambra Court is the top level of the Cloister Wing and is named for the Alhambra Suite, a portion of which can be seen to the left of this photograph. Directly in front, facing north, is the Carmel Tower, which overlooks the southwest corner of Sixth and Orange Streets. This area served as one of many "getaway" spots in the Mission Inn, where people could go to relax and enjoy the ambience. (Courtesy Mission Inn Museum.)

Four

THE SPANISH WING
1914

SPANISH WING AND PATIO, C. 1918. The Spanish Wing was the third wing of the hotel, completed in 1914. This L-shaped structure enclosed and created the Spanish Patio, which is the interior courtyard/restaurant in the hotel. This view looks west from the Garden of the Bells. Instead of romanticizing or copying Mission architecture, Frank Miller hired famous Southern California architect Myron Hunt to design this new wing using more traditional Spanish architecture, hence the name. The Spanish Wing was the last major construction project at the Mission Inn for over 15 years. (Courtesy Steve Lech.)

Glenwood Mission Inn, Riverside, California.

SPANISH WING AND PATIO, C. 1925. The Spanish Wing added two very important elements to the Mission Inn—more rooms and an outdoor dining area. The additional rooms were needed due to the approaching Pan-Pacific Exposition, which was to be held simultaneously in San Diego and San Francisco. Many visitors would be passing through Riverside, and Miller wanted to be able to accommodate them. Similarly, due to his guests' desire to enjoy the climate of Southern California, it made sense to design an outdoor dining area where guests could eat in comfort. (Courtesy Steve Lech.)

SPANISH PATIO, 1930s. Early Mission Inn curator Francis Borton described the Spanish Patio in his *Handbook of the Mission Inn*: "There is no one feature of the Inn that is so distinctively Moorish and Spanish as this cool green patio with its arched openings, grilled gates and windows, Alhambra balconies, tinkling marble fountain, grinning gargoyles, orange trees, feathery palms, pavement of cool red tiles and the gorgeous plumaged Brazilian Macaws, or "huacamayas" swinging on their perches in the shadow of the old Alamo, or cottonwood. And what a delightful place for lunch or dinner (al fresco) . . . it is then that dark-eyed Spanish senoritas, in the costumes of Andalusia, carry us far, far away from the hurry and rush of our restless American life." (Both courtesy Mission Inn Museum.)

SPANISH WING CONSTRUCTION, 1913. These two views show the early construction of the Spanish Wing. The top photograph is taken from the Cloister wing looking at the Garden of the Bells and the eventual Spanish Patio. The bottom view is looking north and shows the foundation work and some of the buildings across Sixth Street from the Mission Inn. Frank Miller kept many workers employed when he added to his hotel, often making impromptu changes to the original plans, adding to the cost and time it took to complete the various construction projects. (Both courtesy Riverside Metropolitan Museum.)

SPANISH ART GALLERY, LATE 1910s. Frank Miller envisioned Riverside as a center for Spanish art, and to accomplish this, he constructed the Spanish Art Gallery as part of the Spanish Wing. At its dedication on December 31, 1914, it housed a display of several Spanish paintings, some old, some reproductions. By 1916, the Spanish Arts Society of California had been formed and held its meeting in the Spanish Art Gallery, where Miller had secured a display of $1.5 million worth of paintings from New York by "old Spanish masters." In later years, the Spanish Art Gallery continued to be a place of artistic display and repose, and it continues to be so by displaying many of the paintings within the hotel's collection. (Both courtesy Mission Inn Museum.)

SPANISH DINING ROOM, C. 1920. One important feature of the Spanish Wing was the addition of the Spanish Dining Room, which added greatly to the Inn's seating capacity for meals. Now guests could have their meals in the new room or just outside in the Spanish Patio. Here a formal table is set for a function in the new dining room. This new area supplemented the California Dining Room. (Courtesy Mission Inn Museum.)

PREPARATIONS FOR JAPANESE FRIENDSHIP DAY CELEBRATION, MAY 10, 1926. Frank Miller hosted several banquets in observance of various foreign holidays. This photograph shows the preparations for Japanese Friendship Day in 1926, which was one of many such occasions during the 1920s and early 1930s. Note the waitresses in kimonos—Frank Miller owned several himself and was often seen wearing them. (Courtesy Riverside Metropolitan Museum.)

WEDDING PARTY IN BRIDAL NOOK, 1920s. The Bridal Nook was located just to the right of the entrance to the Spanish Art Gallery and was used extensively for banquets such as the one pictured above. (Courtesy Riverside Metropolitan Museum.)

SAN PASQUAL KITCHEN, 1920s. Even the kitchen in the hotel served as a place of display. Balconies were incorporated to allow guests to view the inner workings of the kitchen. Here guests were treated to Spanish coats of arms, Chinese carvings, and hand-painted murals depicting the history of California. As in all hotels, the kitchen is a hub of activity, and the Mission Inn was no exception. (Courtesy Mission Inn Museum.)

FUJI KAN ROOM, 1926. As Frank Miller grew older, he became increasingly interested in Asian art and artifacts. Although several pieces graced the hotel from time to time, it was not until 1926 that a specific room was dedicated to their display. At that time, the Fuji Kan room was added on the first floor just over the California and Spanish Dining Rooms. As can be seen, there were many fine examples of Asian art displayed here. Artifact rooms such as the Fuji Kan greatly interested many of the Inn's guests, who became enthralled by the sheer magnitude of the Mission Inn's collections. (Courtesy Mission Inn Museum.)

FUJI KAN ROOM DISPLAY, LATE 1920S. This is one of many displays of small Asian statuary that were common in the Fuji Kan. It was Frank Miller's desire to continually change the displays in the Mission Inn so that there would always be something new and interesting for his guests and the public to enjoy. (Courtesy Riverside Metropolitan Museum.)

MISSION INN ANNEX, LATE 1920S. The Mission Inn Annex is located across from the main hotel on Sixth Street. This structure was originally used as living quarters for the Inn's staff, which were brought in from various locales throughout the region. Initially the staff was housed on the back of the lot in the old Glenwood buildings, but that became impractical as building continued. (Courtesy Riverside Metropolitan Museum.)

ANTON CLOCK AND AUTHOR'S ROW, LATE 1920S. The clock tower on the left is one of the most visible items in the Spanish Patio. It dates to 1709 and is called the Anton Clock after the one in Walter Dyer's story "The Vision of Anton the Clock Maker." Since 1952, a series of five figures has worked with the clock on a turntable. To the right of the clock tower is Author's Row, which consists of six large suites, five of which are named for authors who visited the Inn at various times between 1928 and the 1940s. From left to right, the rooms are named for Carrie Jacobs Bond, Henry Van Dyke, Harold Bell Wright, Joseph Crosby Lincoln, and Zona Gale. The suite on the far right is the Frank Miller Suite. (Courtesy Mission Inn Museum.)

ANTON CLOCK FIGURES, 1950s. These five figures can be seen on the turntable just below the clock and rotate on the quarter hour. They are a California bear, a California American Indian, Juan Bautista de Anza (Spanish explorer who camped in what became Riverside), St. Francis, and Fr. Junipero Serra. These figures were installed by Allis Miller Hutchings in 1952. (Courtesy Mission Inn Museum.)

INTERIOR, CARRIE JACOBS BOND ROOM, LATE 1920s. The Author's Row suites were and still are among the largest of the suites available at the Mission Inn. This upper-most portion of the Spanish Wing was designed by Riverside architect G. Stanley Wilson, who departed from using poured reinforced concrete and instead used hollow tile brick. The Gothic influence added a completely new dimension to the varying architecture of the Mission Inn. (Courtesy Mission Inn Museum.)

MISSION INN ADVERTISING AUTOMOBILE, C. 1920. Frank Miller used every method possible to advertise his hotel, no matter how novel it was. Here is an automobile with a banner. Cars such as this were driven throughout Southern California to make people aware of the Mission Inn. The banner reads "Mission Inn / Riverside California / The Hotel with a Personality / Memories of Spanish Romance / Stop There / On Your Way to Los Angeles." (Courtesy Mission Inn Museum.)

Five

THE ROTUNDA WING
1931

ROTUNDA WING, MID-1940S. The Rotunda Wing, the last wing of the hotel, was completed in 1931. Designed by architect G. Stanley Wilson, it was made almost entirely of poured reinforced concrete. As the hotel business changed, Frank Miller added more commercial space to his hotel. The Rotunda Wing added only 14 hotel rooms but included office space, a larger wedding chapel, more display rooms, and more banquet space. (Courtesy Mission Inn Museum.)

Rotunda Construction, 1931. Workers are pictured here in the Rotunda during its construction. The Rotunda became the commercial corner of the Mission Inn, housing professional offices. At the beginning of the Great Depression, construction of the new Rotunda Wing was considered a boon to local workers and craftsmen, who were engaged for more than two years on this final phase of the Mission Inn. The plaque in front of the workers is an advertisement for Rotunda architect G. Stanley Wilson. (Courtesy Mission Inn Museum.)

ROTUNDA INTERIOR, EARLY 1930S. The interior of the Rotunda is an open cylindrical court 33 feet across and six stories high, including the basement. The railings inside the court are wrought iron and incorporate bell motifs, initials of Spanish explorers, and, on the top row, initials of some of the California missions. Tile coats of arms representing various countries of the world reflect Frank Miller's involvement in the international peace movement that began during World War I. In fact, when opened, the Rotunda was termed the Rotunda International. (Courtesy Mission Inn Museum.)

ST. FRANCIS ATRIO, MID-1930S. The St. Francis Atrio is a small patio in the Rotunda Wing. The Atrio was designed to look like the central square of a little Spanish town. Among its treasures is the Fliers' Wall, the Bacchus Fountain, and the St. Joseph's Arcade facing Sixth Street. Many have seen the small bridge over Sixth Street that connects the Mission Inn to the Mission Inn Annex. This bridge is connected to the St. Francis Atrio and would be just outside the view of this photograph on the right. The bridge was meant for Mission Inn staff—they could enter the atrio and immediately head downstairs to the service areas. (Courtesy Mission Inn Museum.)

BACCHUS FOUNTAIN, MID-1930s. This fountain stands in the center of the St. Francis Atrio. It is a copy of the fountain from the city square in Prato, Italy. (Courtesy Mission Inn Museum.)

ST. FRANCIS ATRIO AND CHAPEL, MID-1930s. Impressive double doors of carved Mexican mahogany allowed guests to enter the chapel from the atrio. Each door was actually a set of two doors. Each of the large doors that open inward has a smaller middle door that opens outward. Frank Miller saw similar doors in old Spanish churches while on a trip to Europe. (Courtesy Mission Inn Museum.)

St. Francis Chapel, Mid-1930s. The St. Francis Wedding Chapel was built to provide a larger room to accommodate the growing number of weddings held at the Mission Inn. The 100-seat chapel, with its beautiful gold altar, stained-glass and mosaic Tiffany windows, and carved wood choir stalls constructed on the premises, immediately made the room a popular venue for memorable weddings. Since its opening in 1932, the St. Francis Chapel has hosted thousands of weddings. Many guests mistake this room for a church. Despite its appearance, the room is not and has never been a church. (Courtesy Steve Lech.)

RAYAS ALTAR, EARLY 1930s. This beautiful altar was constructed for the chapel of the Marquis de Rayes in Guanajuato, Mexico, in the early 1700s. The altar was made of carved Mexican cedar covered with gold leaf and was built in sections and held together with wooden pegs. Frank Miller purchased the altar, sight unseen, in the early 1920s and placed it in the Spanish Art Gallery until the St. Francis Chapel was constructed in 1931. (Courtesy Mission Inn Museum.)

ROSE WINDOW, 1940s. This rose window is one of eight stained-glass and mosaic windows originally made by Louis Comfort Tiffany for the Madison Square Presbyterian Church in New York City. This window has the words "Hast Thou Made Them All" in the center and is surrounded by scenes of the four seasons. (Courtesy Joan Hall.)

GALLERIA, 1930s. The Galleria is 100 feet long by 25 feet wide. It has a 20-foot-high ceiling crisscrossed with concrete beams painted to look like they are wood. This room was primarily a gallery used to display paintings and other artifacts. At the end of the room is the second rose window from the set of Tiffany widows, the rest of which are in the St. Francis Chapel. (Courtesy Mission Inn Museum.)

GARDEN OF THE SKY, 1950s. Located on the top floor of the Rotunda Wing, this patio area with a tile pool was given the picturesque name of Garden of the Sky. It is the only area of the Rotunda Wing to house hotel rooms. The room at the far end is the old Bridal Suite, also known as the Anne Cameron Room, named for a local short-story writer. (Courtesy Mission Inn Museum.)

HALL OF THE GODS, 1930s. This area was actually a wide hallway used to access the Oriental areas of the Mission Inn. Cases were installed to display dolls and other treasures purchased on trips to Europe and Asia or given to the family as gifts. Here is a display of some of the many dolls in the collection. (Courtesy Mission Inn Museum.)

DOLL COLLECTION, LATE 1920s. Frank Miller's two granddaughters, Isabella and Helen Hutchings, began a doll collection that grew to include dolls from all over the world. Many guests of the Mission Inn contributed to the collection over the years. (Courtesy Steve Lech.)

COURT OF THE ORIENT, EARLY 1930S. In order to incorporate more cultures of the world into the Mission Inn, Frank Miller added an Asian influence in the Rotunda Wing. The outside area pictured above, dubbed the Court of the Orient, displayed statuary, many potted plants, and a fishpond, all designed to suggest a serene Oriental oasis. In addition, hotel rooms partially surround the courtyard, which really only lasted throughout the 1930s. In 1939, this area became the Lea Lea Room but was returned to the Court of the Orient during the renovation. To the right of this photograph is the entrance to the Ho-O-Kan Room. (Courtesy Mission Inn Museum.)

HO-O-KAN ROOM, EARLY 1930S. The Ho-O-Kan Room opened onto the Oriental court. This room, together with the earlier Fuji Kan, was used to display much of Frank Miller's Oriental artwork. The most prominent object in the room is the gold and lacquer Buddha. The figure is over seven feet tall and dates to the late 19th century. The Mission Inn acquired it in the 1920s. (Courtesy Mission Inn Museum.)

JAPANESE BRONZE WATER DRAGON, 1930S. This bronze sculpture is a Japanese water dragon (Note the great wave of water coming out of its mouth). It is almost six and a half feet tall and probably dates to the late 19th century. To many Asians, dragons symbolize strength, abundance, prosperity, and good fortune. (Courtesy Mission Inn Museum.)

AMISTAD DOME, LATE 1930S. The Amistad (friendship) Dome rises on the northwest corner of the Rotunda Wing. Covered in glazed Mexican tile and proudly displaying the raincross symbol, the dome rests over a 20-foot-wide round room that has been called the University Club and the Anne Cameron Room. The view from this perspective and others was no coincidence—Frank Miller made sure that his guests could view as much of the greater Riverside area as possible so they would realize its potential and invest their money in land, orange groves, or businesses. (Courtesy Mission Inn Museum.)

Six

FACES AT THE MISSION INN

VISIT OF PRES. THEODORE ROOSEVELT, MAY 8, 1903. President Roosevelt spent the night of May 7 at the new Glenwood Mission Inn as a guest of Frank Miller. At 7:30 on the morning of the 8th, just before his departure, the president helped in the transplanting of one of the two parent navel orange trees into the courtyard of the new hotel (the other being placed at the corner of Arlington and Magnolia Avenues). This tree would be a popular tourist site for another 20 years until it died. (Courtesy Steve Lech.)

MISSION INN GUESTS, C. 1912. These two women demonstrate the formal nature of staying at the hotel. It must be remembered that the Mission Inn was a hostel devoted to the wealthy. Virtually everything, from meals to concerts to outings and even moments of relaxation called for formal dress, and picture-taking in the Garden of the Bells, as these two are doing, was no exception. By today's much more relaxed standards, these two may seem overly elegant, but dress such as this was expected in Edwardian times. (Both courtesy Joan Hall.)

BOOKER T. WASHINGTON AND FRANK MILLER ATOP MOUNT RUBIDOUX, MARCH 23, 1914. Noted orator and educator Booker T. Washington arrived in Riverside to give speeches at the First Congregational Church and the Second Baptist Church. Afterward, he was whisked away by Frank Miller who took him to Mount Rubidoux to see the greater Riverside area. That evening, Miller invited Mr. Washington to give a final speech in the Inn's Music Room. This speech, outlining the need for education for America's black population, was well received, and Miller and Washington became friends. Unfortunately, Booker T. Washington died the next year. However, he and his visit are commemorated in the bust that is situated next to the campanario in the Mission Inn courtyard. (Courtesy Mission Inn Museum.)

EDDIE PEABODY, DECEMBER 1930. Eddie Peabody was a famous vaudeville musician who mastered more than 30 instruments, although he was best known for playing the banjo. Peabody toured throughout the country, but when he visited the Mission Inn in the mid-1920s, he decided Riverside was where he would live. He purchased an orange grove, settled in Riverside, and spent many nights giving recitals and playing for benefit concerts at the Mission Inn. (Courtesy Mission Inn Museum.)

CAPT. EDWARD "EDDIE" RICKENBACKER, C. 1918. World War I air ace Eddie Rickenbacker visited the Mission Inn on two occasions, the first in June 1919 and the second in March 1942. It was during the first visit that he penned this photograph, "To Mrs. Alice Richardson, With Every Best Wish, Capt. Eddie Rickenbacker, June 25-19." Twenty-three years later, on March 20, 1942, Rickenbacker returned, and this time helped place his wings on the Famous Fliers' Wall. (Courtesy Mission Inn Museum.)

VISIT OF CROWN PRINCE GUSTAVUS ADOLPHUS OF SWEDEN, JULY 21, 1926. Crown Prince Gustavus Adolphus, together with his wife, Princess Louise, toured Riverside's extensive orange groves and then dined at the Inn at a banquet held in their honor. He said of his surroundings: "Of all the hotels I have visited in the United States, I never have seen one to compare with the Mission Inn." Crown Prince Gustavus later became King Gustavus VI Adolphus, reigning from 1950 to 1973. (Courtesy Mission Inn Museum.)

GERTRUDE RIDGEWAY, C. 1920. Gertrude Ridgeway was a musician and dancer who appeared often in and around the Mission Inn. As shown in this photograph, she was often dressed as a Spanish dancer performing for guests. Other times, she would play violin and accompany various Mission Inn musicians in the Music Room. (Courtesy Mission Inn Museum.)

TOM MIX AT WEDDING, LATE 1920s. Silent movie-era cowboy Tom Mix is pictured (just left of the child) in this wedding gathering in the Mission Inn's courtyard. It was not uncommon for movie stars and other famous people to come to the Mission Inn to escape the hustle of their daily lives. (Courtesy Riverside Metropolitan Museum.)

CARRIE JACOBS BOND IN SUITE, C. 1930. Carrie Jacobs Bond was an artist and songwriter who visited the Inn on several occasions. She was probably best known for her song "I Love You Truly," which was often heard at weddings. After a visit to Mount Rubidoux in 1909, she penned a poem entitled "A Perfect Day." She later set it to music and changed the title to "The End of a Perfect Day." That very popular song became the song of the Mission Inn and is still heard there today. (Courtesy Mission Inn Museum.)

WILL ROGERS IN THE COURT OF THE BIRDS, 1933. Will Rogers, the well-known cowboy, comedian, and philosopher, was a frequent visitor to the Mission Inn in the 1920s and 1930s. In 1933, he spent time at the hotel during the filming of *State Fair*, in which he played opposite Janet Gaynor. During his visit, Rogers continued to write his well-loved newspaper column and said of the Mission Inn, "It is the most unique hotel in America. It's a monastery, a museum, a fine hotel, a home, a boardinghouse, a mission, an art gallery and an aviator's shrine. It combines the best features of all of the above. If you are ever in any part of California, don't miss this famous Mission Inn in Riverside." (Courtesy Mission Inn Museum.)

VISIT OF PRINCE AND PRINCESS KAYA, AUGUST 31, 1934. Japanese prince Tsunerori Kaya, first cousin to Emperor Hirohito, and his wife, Toshiko, arrived in Riverside after an extensive trip throughout the United States. As guests of Frank Miller, they were treated to a special luncheon and a tour of the hotel, which included the Court of the Orient and the Ho-O-Kan Room housing a part of Miller's extensive Asian artifact collection. (Courtesy Mission Inn Museum.)

AMELIA EARHART WITH DEWITT HUTCHINGS, FEBRUARY 1936. Famed aviatrix Amelia Earhart was an occasional visitor to the Mission Inn, but it was not until February 3, 1936, that she initialed her wings and installed them on the Fliers' Wall. At that time, she posed for several photographs, including this one with DeWitt Hutchings and Napoleon the macaw. (Courtesy Mission Inn Museum.)

MAJ. ALBERT STEVENS AT THE FLIERS' WALL, JANUARY 12, 1937. Maj. Stevens commanded the first airship (a balloon) to enter the stratosphere. The flight took place on November 11, 1935. On January 12, 1937, Major Stevens visited the Mission Inn at the request of DeWitt Hutchings and placed his wings on the wall, the 37th person to do so. (Courtesy Mission Inn Museum.)

HELEN PAICH FORBES, 1947. This photograph of Helen Paich Forbes shows her in the Court of the Birds in one of the swings that hung from the pergola. Helen came with her daughter to Riverside in the 1940s, and her first job was as a waitress at the Mission Inn. The daughter fondly remembers her mother's beautiful, elaborate Spanish-style uniform. (Courtesy Catherine Manion.)

DALE EVANS, EDDIE CANTOR, AND MARY ASTOR WITH DEWITT HUTCHINGS, C. 1943. During World War II, the Mission Inn played host to several war bond rallies. War bond rallies were meant to stimulate the purchase of bonds to finance the war effort, and they were usually star-studded affairs. Dale Evans (western movie star and wife of Roy Rogers), Eddie Cantor (comedic singer and stage actor), and Mary Astor (movie actress popular in the 1930s and 1940s) are pictured here with Inn manager DeWitt Hutchings on their visit to the Mission Inn for such a war bond rally. (Courtesy Mission Inn Museum.)

JUDY GARLAND AND DAVID ROSE, 1942. Film actress Judy Garland, best known as Dorothy in the Wizard of Oz, and musician David Rose were secretly married in July 1941. Unable to have a honeymoon directly after their wedding, they decided to go to the Palm Springs area early in 1942 and stopped briefly at the Mission Inn. Here they are pictured dining in the Spanish Patio. (Courtesy Mission Inn Museum.)

GLORIA SWANSON AND CHARLES WALTERS AT MISSION INN POOL, 1949. Gloria Swanson, a veteran actress of both silent and sound pictures, relaxes here beside the Mission Inn pool with director Charles Walters. Many times, well-known people would come to the Mission Inn to get away from the crowds and know that, for the most part, they could be left in relative peace. (Courtesy Mission Inn Museum.)

MAY SPILLER, C. 1960. One of the most flamboyant characters to have graced the Mission Inn in later years was May Spiller. Hired originally in 1939 as the Inn's social director, she soon took it upon herself to offer tours of the hotel to interested guests. As the years went by, both she and her tours became more and more popular. Her trademark was her large-brimmed, flowered hats, custom designed by Walter Florel of New York, who sent her some of his latest creations every year. Many a guest enjoyed touring with May Spiller and listening to her stories of Frank Miller, the hotel, and its many artifacts. After her daily tours, Spiller would retire to one of the Inn's bars to have a drink. May Spiller conducted tours of the hotel until she turned 90 in 1966. She died two years later. (Courtesy Mission Inn Museum.)

MAY SPILLER CONDUCTING TOUR, LATE 1950S. Unfortunately, by most accounts, May Spiller's stories may have been rooted more in a desire to impress guests than in fact. This may account for many of the myths and stories that are still believed about the Inn but are not true. May Spiller, though, was certainly not the only person guilty of this. (Courtesy Mission Inn Museum.)

MISSION INN TOUR, 1955. For several years, tour guests of the Inn were photographed in the St. Francis Atrio, with an opportunity to purchase the photograph afterward. Pictured here in the center of the photograph are Walter and Mary Lech, the author's grandparents, enjoying a tour of the Inn in 1955 while on a trip to Southern California from Framingham, Massachusetts. (Courtesy Steve Lech.)

RICHARD AND PAT NIXON, 1952. Richard Nixon visited the Mission Inn frequently as a child. He and his wife, Pat, were married in the Presidential Suite on June 21, 1940. Twelve years later, while they were staying in the hotel, he received the telegram informing him that he had been chosen as Gen. Dwight Eisenhower's running mate for the 1952 election. At that time, the picture to the left was taken in the Alhambra Suite. (Courtesy Mission Inn Museum.)

BETTE DAVIS MARRIAGE TO WILLIAM GRANT SHERRY, NOVEMBER 29, 1945. Bette Davis and William Sherry were married in the St. Francis Chapel after officials at Laguna's St. Mary's Episcopal Church would not allow her to be married in the church due to her 1938 divorce from Harmon O. Nelson Jr. The plan was for the couple to be married at the Mission Inn, have their reception there, then go to the Smoke Tree Ranch in Palm Springs and eventually to Mexico City. (Courtesy Mission Inn Museum.)

Seven
THE MISSION INN SINCE FRANK MILLER

EL MUNDO COCKTAIL LOUNGE, LATE 1930s. The El Mundo was the first dedicated bar/lounge in the Mission Inn. Frank Miller had been a strict temperance adherent, and as such, there were no bars in the Mission Inn while he was alive. After his death, his grandchildren applied for a liquor license and opened a series of bars/lounges in the hotel. The El Mundo was located on the first floor in the old Fuji Kan Room. (Courtesy Mission Inn Museum.)

LEA LEA ROOM, C. 1940. The Lea Lea Room was opened on December 16, 1939, by Frank and Isabella Hutchings. It was a dinner/dance club that had a south-seas motif, as evidenced by the bamboo furniture, palm fronds, etc. Pictured here is the dance floor surrounded by cocktail tables. The Lea Lea Room was removed during the renovation of the hotel. (Courtesy Mission Inn Museum.)

LEA LEA ROOM BAR, MID-1950S. The bar area was located in the Ho-O-Kan room, which retained many of the Asian artifacts from its former years. Note the large Buddha statue behind the bar and the Chinese reverse-glass painted lanterns above. These artifacts still exist in the modern Ho-O-Kan room. The dance floor in the previous view would be to the right of this photograph. (Courtesy Mission Inn Museum.)

WACS AT THE MISSION INN, 1940S.
During World War II, the Mission Inn was a hub of activity, serving as a popular gathering spot and nightclub for service personnel from the many military bases that dotted inland Southern California. Here two WACS walk along one of the overlooks of the Spanish Patio. (Courtesy Mission Inn Museum.)

USO FUNCTION, EARLY 1940S. Due to the influx of military personnel to the Riverside area during World War II, the Mission Inn served as a center for the USO, which, as now, sought to give morale, welfare, and recreation to those in uniform. Here is one such gathering of the USO in the banquet room to the west of the California Dining Room. (Courtesy Riverside Metropolitan Museum.)

DEMOLITION OF "OLD ADOBE," 1948. As part of the 1948 modernization of the hotel undertaken by Allis and DeWitt Hutchings, the "Old Adobe" structure that had been the beginning of the hotel in the 1870s was torn down to make way for a swimming pool. In the postwar era of automobile travel and the decline in usage of "destination" hotels such as the Mission Inn, it was imperative that modern hotels have a swimming pool. The Hutchings realized this, and the "Old Adobe" was sacrificed for this reason. (Courtesy Mission Inn Museum.)

MISSION INN SWIMMING POOL, EARLY 1950S. The Mission Inn pool became a popular attraction not only for hotel guests but also for residents of Riverside. Residents could pay an annual fee and have use of the pool anytime they wanted. During the 1950s and 1960s, a Mission Inn Swim Club attracted many residents, especially when the Inn hired noted swimmer Steve Petrick to be its swimming instructor. Many Riversiders learned to swim at the Inn. (Courtesy Mission Inn Museum.)

EAST FACADE, MISSION INN, C. 1947. This view, taken from the parking lot of the old library, shows the east facade of the Mission Inn shortly before its first modernization. (Courtesy Mission Inn Museum.)

MISSION INN LOBBY, C. 1948. In 1948, with the Mission Inn suffering a financial decline after the war, Allis and DeWitt Hutchings decided to "modernize" the hotel. As seen in this photograph, many of the Arts and Crafts furnishings were removed and a more modern look was achieved. At the same time, the Orange Street entrance to the lobby was created, as seen in the center of this photograph. Unfortunately, the modernization of the hotel could not surmount the wave of suburbanization that was enveloping Southern California, and despite the best efforts, the Inn would see many years of financial hardship in its future. (Courtesy Mission Inn Museum.)

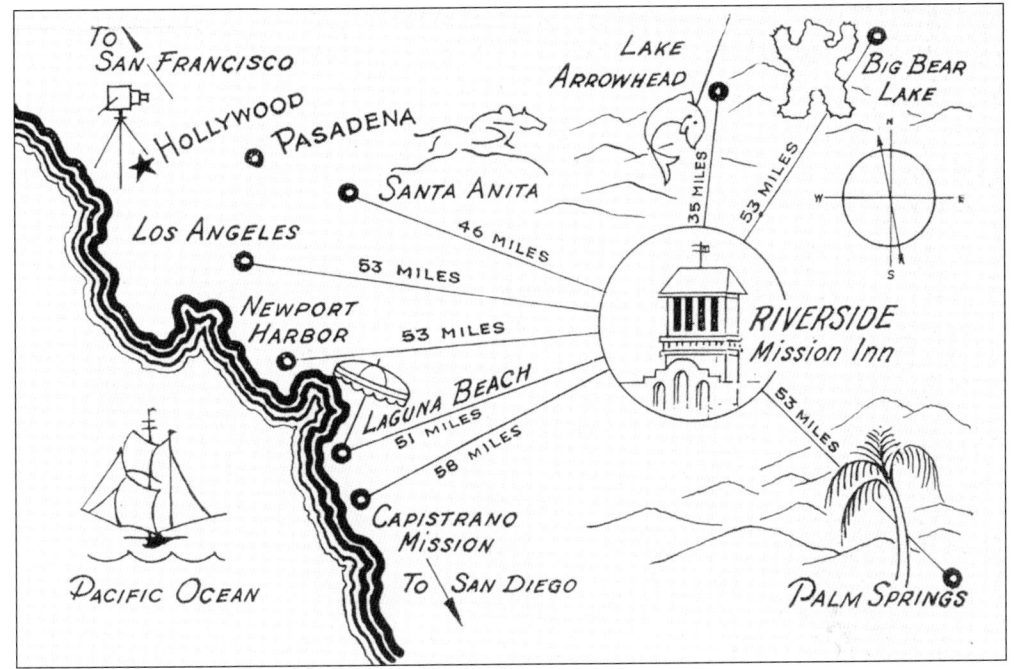

MISSION INN LOCATION MAP, 1949. By the time of this advertisement during the postwar-automobile travel boom, the Mission Inn was no longer attracting people who wanted to spend weeks in one place. Therefore, ads such as this were used to show people that various other Southern California amenities, such as the beaches, mountains, and deserts were easily accessible with a drive of a few miles. (Courtesy Mission Inn Museum.)

FILMING OF THE FIRST LEGION, 1950. The Mission Inn has been the setting of many movies over the years, and The First Legion, starring Charles Boyer and William Demarest, is one of the more memorable. In the film, the Inn is portrayed as a Jesuit seminary in which Boyer investigates the alleged occurrence of a miracle. The film is a good time capsule for how the Mission Inn appeared in the waning days of the Hutchings' ownership. (Courtesy Joan Hall.)

MISSION INN LOBBY, 1950s. Starting in 1956, another more thorough modernization of the Mission Inn began under Ben Swig and involved removing most vestiges of its past and replacing them with modern furnishings, colors, and decorating techniques. Note the minimalist nature of this lobby versus the lobby of the Miller years. Many have derided Swig for his modernization, especially given that he removed and destroyed so much of the original Arts and Crafts furnishings, including original Stickley examples. However, the zeitgeist of the 1950s was vastly different than today. People looked to the future and were not interested in preserving the past. Most people today, although shocked by the contrast of the Swig years versus the Miller years, realize that it is through Swig's tenacity and regard for the hotel that Riverside even has the hotel today, given that there was a myriad of people who once saw the Mission Inn as a "white elephant" whose days had come and gone. (Courtesy Mission Inn Museum.)

CALIFORNIA DINING ROOM, LATE 1950S. Ben Swig's modernization of the Mission Inn was total, as evidenced here in this photograph of the California Dining Room. Muted pastel colors replaced the white paint and dark woodwork of the original room. New carpeting, drapes, and modern lighting fixtures were added to bring the hotel "up to date." (Courtesy Mission Inn Museum.)

PRESIDENTIAL LOUNGE, 1958. In 1957, Ben Swig converted the old Presidential Suite into a bar and lounge and renamed it the Presidential Lounge, as it is still known today. A bar was placed where the two bedrooms had been (in the background), and the old sitting room was converted into the lounge, complete with piano bar, as seen in the foreground. The Presidential Lounge continues to be a popular gathering/meeting spot in the Inn. (Courtesy Mission Inn Museum.)

SQUIRE ARMS RESTAURANT/ CLUB, C. 1958. The Squire Arms was a thoroughly new and modern restaurant and club patterned after the Squire Room in Ben Swig's Fairmount Hotel. This was a popular place for businessmen during the late 1950s and 1960s. Previously the area had been a banquet room—today it is the location of Duane's Prime Steaks and Seafood Restaurant. (Courtesy Mission Inn Museum.)

SQUIRE ARMS SIGN, C. 1958. This sign hung on Main Street above the passageway leading to the courtyard. (Courtesy Mission Inn Museum.)

MAIN STREET AND MISSION INN WESTERN FACADE, EARLY 1960S. By the time of this photograph, then-owner Ben Swig had thoroughly upgraded the hotel to try to rid it of its "old" image. Several non-hotel owned businesses had rented space in the Mission Inn, including Banks Drug Store and the Book Nook. Unfortunately for the Mission Inn and Riverside's downtown area in general, many businesses were leaving for newer quarters in suburban shopping areas such as the Brockton Arcade and the Riverside Plaza. In just a few years, Main Street, as pictured above, would be converted into a pedestrian mall. (Courtesy Mission Inn Museum.)

MISSION WING RENOVATION, C. 1986. By the 1980s, the Mission Inn had deteriorated to a point where either renovation or demolition had to occur. Luckily a renovation was started in 1985. During the renovation, it was discovered that the Mission Wing was constructed almost entirely of timbers and unreinforced masonry. Many of the timbers had rotted or cracked and unreinforced masonry is a hazard in earthquake-prone Southern California. During the renovation, modern reinforcing techniques were used to greatly strengthen the building and make it conform to modern building codes while at the same time maintaining the historic integrity of the building. The renovation of a building of this magnitude was a tremendous undertaking given all of the challenges of the project. The view above shows the unreinforced masonry encountered just to the west of the main entrance to the hotel. (Courtesy Mission Inn Museum.)

MISSION WING RENOVATION, C. 1987. During the renovation, it was found that some of the foundation had been undercut by leaking water and sewer pipes. This section, in the California Dining Room, had to be sequentially lifted and placed on jacks so that the foundation could be repaired. This view shows much the same photograph as the previous view, near the main entrance. (Courtesy Mission Inn Hotel.)

MISSION INN TERMITE TENTING, LATE JUNE–EARLY JULY OF 1987. As one of the many things that had to be done to the Mission Inn during its renovation, the entire building was tented for termite fumigation, as pictured above. This fete took over 400 tarpaulins to cover the Inn, making quite a spectacle. At that time, it was featured in the *Guinness Book of World Records* as the largest termite fumigation tent. (Courtesy Mission Inn Museum.)

CONSTRUCTION OF NEW SEVENTH STREET ARCHES, C. 1988. Both the arches along Seventh Street (now Mission Inn Avenue) and the campanario in the courtyard were determined to be too far deteriorated to restore in their original state. Therefore, they were removed and new ones built to the original specifications were constructed during the renovation. The top photograph shows the new main structure of the arches, while the bottom shows the arches before being stuccoed. Many of the original bricks were saved, and for several years after these photographs were taken, a person received a brick with a paid membership to the Mission Inn Foundation. (Above photograph courtesy Mission Inn Hotel; below photograph courtesy Mission Inn Museum.)

RENOVATION OF THE CLOISTER AND SPANISH WINGS, C. 1988. The non–Mission Wing portions of the hotel were, as a rule, built of poured, reinforced concrete, and withstood the test of time better than the Mission Wing. The scaffolding on Sixth Street was placed so that this portion of the building could be inspected thoroughly for any damage and the building could be cleaned. This scaffolding remained for several months at the Mission Inn. (Courtesy Mission Inn Museum.)

RENOVATION OF THE ST. FRANCIS CHAPEL ALTAR, C. 1988. No artifact or piece of the building was exempt from a thorough examination during the renovation, and the altar in the St. Francis Chapel was no exception. Scaffolding was erected just in front of the altar as pictured above, and the altar was examined to determine its condition. Luckily it was found to be in good condition, and it was given a thorough cleaning before removal of the scaffolding. (Courtesy Mission Inn Museum.)

MISSION INN DOCENT GRADUATION, MAY 1989. Since 1987, the Mission Inn Foundation has trained hundreds of area volunteers to be Mission Inn docents. Docents go through nearly nine months of training in history, architecture, and art in order to conduct tours of the hotel. Beginning in January 1993, the docents have led thousands of visitors through the Mission Inn on a regular basis. The authors are standing towards the center of the above photograph. (Courtesy Mission Inn Museum.)

"SIDEWALK STROLL" TOUR, C. 1990. Beginning in the summer of 1989, eager Mission Inn docents began a series of "Sidewalk Stroll" tours around the perimeter of the closed Mission Inn. These tours were free to the public, and although none of the interior could be explored, people anxiously went on the tours anticipating the day when the Mission Inn would reopen. (Courtesy Mission Inn Museum.)

DUANE R. ROBERTS, 2006. Duane R. Roberts is an entrepreneur and investor who was born and raised in Riverside. After making his family's food business a success, he turned to investing in real estate and other ventures. On December 24, 1992, he purchased the Mission Inn and reopened it after its seven-and-a-half-year closure. Since then, the Mission Inn has once again risen to national prominence. Under Mr. Roberts's ownership, the Inn operates three award-winning restaurants and continues to host banquets, conventions, scores of weddings, and of course, overnight guests who come to stay in the hotel that continues to be called the "Heart of Riverside." Since Frank Miller was known as the "Master of the Inn," Duane R. Roberts has been termed the "Keeper of the Inn," a fitting title. (Courtesy Entrepreneurial Corporate Group.)

Eight
THE MILLER FAMILY

FRANK MILLER, C. 1880. Here Frank Miller is pictured as a young man, just a few years after he moved to Riverside. It was at about this time that he married Isabella Hardenburg and assumed ownership of the Glenwood Hotel from his father. He would spend the rest of his life, 55 years, operating a hotel in downtown Riverside, all the while promoting the city in any way he could. (Courtesy Mission Inn Museum.)

CHRISTOPHER MILLER, C. 1860S. The patriarch of the Miller family in California, Christopher Columbus (C. C.) Miller had been a captain in the Union Army during the Civil War and was a trained engineer and surveyor who had worked on railroads in Wisconsin and Minnesota. He came to California in search of work and a healthier climate for his ailing wife, Mary. (Courtesy Mission Inn Museum.)

MARY MILLER, C. 1860S. Mary Clark Miller was an Oberlin College graduate and taught school before her marriage. Education was very important to her, and she took it upon herself to make sure her children were well schooled. Her son Frank Miller, though, rejected formal education in lieu of his innate business sense. (Courtesy Mission Inn Museum.)

MILLER CHILDREN, EARLY 1860S. Pictured here, from left to right, are Frank, Emma, and Alice Miller as young children. They were still living in Tomah, Wisconsin, at the time. Ed Miller, the youngest son, had not yet been born at the time of this photograph. (Courtesy Mission Inn Museum.)

ALICE MILLER, MID-1890S. Alice was the younger of Frank Miller's two sisters. She was born in 1860, and in 1885, she married Frank Richardson, who worked at the Glenwood. They soon became the managers of the hotel. After her husband's early death, "Aunt Alice" continued as the day-to-day manager of her brother's hotels, first the Glenwood and then the Mission Inn. (Courtesy Riverside Metropolitan Museum.)

EDWARD MILLER, AUGUST 1896. Edward "Ed" Miller was the youngest of the four Miller children. In addition to helping in the day-to-day operation of the hotel, Ed Miller drove various vehicles, from horse-drawn wagons to automobiles, between the train stations and the hotel, bringing guests to his brother's Glenwood Hotel and later the Mission Inn. (Courtesy Riverside Metropolitan Museum.)

ISABELLA HARDENBURG, C. 1880. Isabella Hardenburg had been a local schoolteacher who boarded with the Miller family. It was Mary Miller's hope that she would be able to tutor Frank Miller, who generally rejected school. That arrangement, however, resulted in the couple's marriage in 1880. (Courtesy Mission Inn Museum.)

MILLER AND NEWMAN FAMILY GATHERING, 1895. The Miller and Newman families are pictured here at the Newman ranch, located at the southwest corner of Market and Fourteenth Streets. Civil engineer Gustavus Newman was Emma Miller's husband and Christopher Miller's business partner. The gathering was in honor of Frank Miller's birthday. Pictured, from left to right, are (first row) the Newman twins; (second row) unidentified, Vera Miller, Stanley Richardson, Gustavus Newman, Isabella Hardenburg Miller, Frank Miller, Marion Clark Miller (Frank's mother), Albert Miller, and Allis Miller; (third row) Mr. Newman, Ralph Newman, Frank Richardson, Alice Miller Richardson, Olive Newman, Emma Newman, Mrs. Ed (Emma) Miller, Ed Miller, and Emma Miller Newman. (Courtesy Mission Inn Museum.)

FRANK AND ALLIS MILLER, 1882.
From the marriage of Frank Miller and Isabella Hardenburg came one daughter, Allis, pictured above with her father in 1882. Young Allis was named for her aunt Alice, but the spelling was changed to avoid confusion. (Courtesy Mission Inn Museum.)

FRANK MILLER AND FAMILY, OCTOBER 1893. In October 1893, Frank Miller, his wife Isabella, and their 11-year-old daughter Allis went to the Chicago World's Fair, where they had the above photograph taken. At this world's fair, Frank Miller saw the wonderful opportunities that awaited wealthy tourists and immediately decided to revamp his hotel into a modern, luxury hotel. (Courtesy Riverside Metropolitan Museum.)

ALLIS MILLER, C. 1908. Allis Miller was the only child of Frank and Isabella Miller. She is pictured here just before her marriage to DeWitt Hutchings in 1909. Allis and DeWitt helped to manage the hotel while her father was alive. After Frank Miller's death in 1935, Allis and DeWitt Hutchings took over ownership and management until they both died in the early 1950s. (Courtesy Riverside Metropolitan Museum.)

DEWITT AND ALLIS HUTCHINGS, C. 1920. The Hutchings are pictured here sitting on the fountain in the Spanish Patio. DeWitt Hutchings was originally from New Jersey and was a graduate of Princeton. He visited the Glenwood during the winter of 1908–1909 where he met Allis Miller. Their 1909 wedding was a quiet affair due to the death the previous year of Allis's mother, Isabella. (Courtesy Riverside Metropolitan Museum.)

FRANK MILLER AND FAMILY MEMBERS, 1911. Here Frank Miller sits next to his second wife, Marion. Across the table is Alice Richardson. The youngster in the carriage is Frank Miller Hutchings, Miller's grandson. Frank Miller's first wife, Isabella Hardenburg Miller, died in 1908 after a short illness. Miller found consolation in his secretary, Marion Clark, who he had hired two years before. Although she was half his age at the time, the two were married in a private ceremony in New York in December 1910. (Courtesy Mission Inn Museum.)

FRANK MILLER AND ALICE RICHARDSON IN COURTYARD, 1910. Frank Miller and his sister Alice Richardson (the Inn's manager) were always seen in or around the hotel making sure their guests were comfortable. In this view, they are in the courtyard with the old careta, an old Mexican-era ox cart that Frank Miller procured early in the Mission Inn's life. It remained in the courtyard for years, adding to the symbolism and charm of the hotel. (Courtesy Riverside Metropolitan Museum.)

FRANK MILLER WITH GRANDCHILDREN, 1915.
Frank Miller is pictured seated with his newest grandchild, Isabella Hutchings. Standing to the right is his grandson Frank Miller Hutchings. Allis Hutchings, his daughter and the mother of the two children, is seated to the left. (Courtesy Mission Inn Museum, Jane Clark Cullen Collection.)

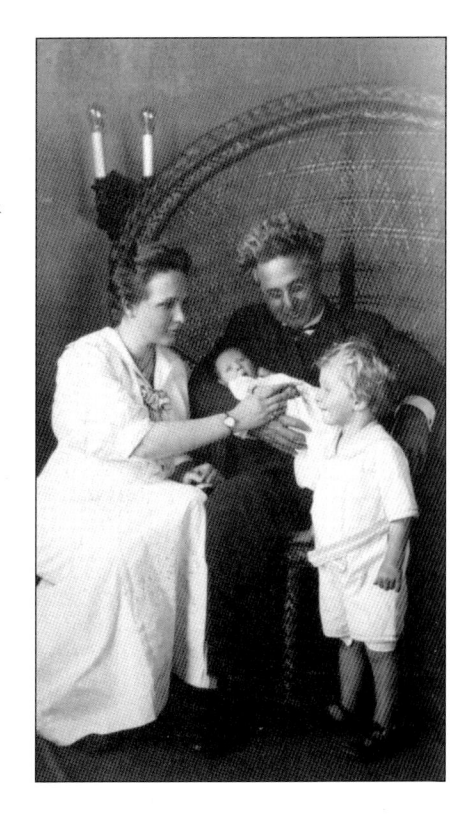

MILLER GRANDCHILDREN AT CASA MARIONA, C. 1923. Casa Mariona was a house built by Frank Miller for his second wife, Marion (hence the name), overlooking the beach at Laguna. This became a popular place for escape for the Miller family. The view above shows the front entrance and the three grandchildren, Frank, Isabella, and Helen, on the entry walk. (Courtesy Mission Inn Museum, Jane Clark Cullen Collection.)

BIBLIOGRAPHY

Borton, Francis. *Handbook of the Mission Inn*. Riverside, CA: Cloister Print Shop, (nd).

Gale, Zona. *Frank Miller of Mission Inn*. New York, NY: D. Appleton-Century Company, 1938.

Hall, Joan. *Through the Doors of the Mission Inn*. Riverside, CA: Highgrove Press, 1996.

———. *Through the Doors of the Mission Inn, Volume II*. Riverside, CA: Highgrove Press, 2000.

Hodgen, Maurice. *More than Decoration: Asian Objects at the Mission Inn*. Riverside, CA Ashburton Publishing, 2004.

Hutchings, Allis Miller. *Dolls and Animals of the World*. Privately printed: (nd).

———. *The Monkey Book*. Riverside, CA: The Mission Inn, 1946.

Hutchings, DeWitt. *Handbook of the Mission Inn*. Riverside, CA: Cloister Print Shop, 1944.

Jarrell Johnson, Kim. *Jurupa*. Charleston, SC: Arcadia Publishing, 2006.

Klotz, Esther. *The Mission Inn: Its History and Artifacts*. Riverside, CA: Rubidoux Printing, 1981.

Lech, Steve. *Along the Old Roads: A History of the Portion of Southern California That Became Riverside County, 1772–1893*. Riverside, CA: Published by the author, 2004.

Lech, Steve. *Resorts of Riverside County*. Charleston, SC: Arcadia Publishing, 2005.

Lech, Steve. *Riverside in Vintage Postcards*. Charleston, SC: Arcadia Publishing, 2005.

Los Angeles Times, various dates.

Parks, Walt. *The Famous Fliers' Wall*. Riverside, CA: Rubidoux Printing, 1986.

Riverside Press, various dates.